I0145613

GOD SEES
GREATNESS NU2

GOD SEES

GREATNESS NU2

Overcoming the Suicide Battle Within

&

31 Days of Fresh Nuggets
for the Hungry in Christ

THERESA C. FRIDAY

God Sees Greatness NU2: Overcoming the Suicide Battle Within

Copyright © 2015 by Theresa C. Friday

All rights reserved. No part of this publication may be reproduced, stored in a retrieval system, or transmitted in any form or by any means electronic, mechanical, photocopying, recording, or otherwise, without the prior written permission of the publisher.

Edited by: Stella Joy

Published by: Theresa C. Friday, Enterprise LLC.

Printed in the United States of America

ISBN: 978-0-692-65690-7

All Scripture quotations, unless otherwise indicated, are taken from the Holy Bible, New International Version®, NIV®. Copyright ©1973, 1978, 1984, 2011 by Biblical, Inc.™ Used by permission of Zondervan. All rights reserved worldwide. *www.zondervan.com.* The "NIV" and "New International Version" are trademarks registered in the United States Patent and Trademark Office by Biblical, Inc.™

Other version used is:
KJV - Kings James Version. Authorized King James Version.

To The Glory Of God.

My first book is dedicated to:

In memory of my mother
Quincess Hall Collins

Father
Joe C. Collins

Husband
Andrew Friday, Jr.

Children
Jeremiah & Jala Friday

My sibling's
Joe Drake Collins
Coretta Collins

My best friend
Kimetta Young McGee

who have always supported me with unwavering love.

Contents

Acknowledgements

With grateful thanks to all who contributed to this book and everyone who has offered encouragement, prayers and a shoulder on which to lean on, I am very grateful.

To all of my friends and family, I love you from the bottom of my heart!

Foreword

Castrate.

To remove or be incapable of reproduction; to edit by omitting or modifying parts that are considered indelicate.

We all at some point in time, have or will have issues in our life that need to be castrated. In other words, we have issues that need to be omitted and incapable of reproduction. However, the only way we will be able to "castrate" these stumbling blocks is by reading, hearing and doing what the word of God is saying to us. We must accept Jesus, and become filled with the Holy Spirit. Many blessings and promises are stored and ready to be released for those who love and do the will of GOD!

This devotional book consists of daily motivational nuggets inspired by the Holy Spirit in order to help you along your journey. In my personal experience of castrating stumbling blocks, I realized that reading the word of God and receiving the Holy Spirit was the only tool that could help me overcome all the adversities in my life. Furthermore, I also found that in order to keep your mind renewed, you must read, listen, hear and then apply what you know to your everyday life. God's word inspires action.

God wants our mind to be free of all those "things" that keep us from focusing on Him and His will for our lives. The enemy desires for our minds to be devoid of peace. We will not always know what to do in every situation, but we can have peace. This book was written to help you walk your daily journey, and so that you have confidence in Jesus. Today, say goodbye to your hidden issues and to the issues that have taken control over your mind. Once you begin to hunger for God's word, He will fill you! The bible teaches me that blessed are they which do hunger and thirst after righteousness for they shall be filled! (Matthew 5:6) So, stay hungry for Christ. Have a receptive heart and allow God to use you the way He wants to use you!

Prepare yourself for mealtime every time you get ready to explore the Word of God ... Nuggets anyone?

Taminko Jones Kelley
Owner of CoolBird Marketing, LLC

My Life, But God's Glory

"My powerless, painful past is now
my Press through Purpose!"

—THERESA C. FRIDAY

"For I know the plans I have for you", declares the
LORD, "plans to prosper you and not to harm you,
plans to give you hope and a future."

—JEREMIAH 29:11 (NIV)

They triumphed over him by the blood of the Lamb
and by the word of their testimony; they did love
their lives so much as to shrink from death.

—REV 12:11 (NIV)

The Struggle, Battle and War

After growing up in an ideal, two-parent family home, my life dramatically changed at the age of ten. My once happy personality became overshadowed by thoughts of unworthiness, isolation, and emotional distress. Not only did I find myself struggling with depression, I was dealing with a double burden, being as young as I was, I was also impacted by my depressed mother. I was forced to become a mini adult, taking over such duties as caring for my younger siblings because my mother was too depressed to function. My mother's battle with depression ended with a suicide attempt. I don't want to relive this horrible moment, she had taken an overdose and was clinging to life, but God saved her. After seeking professional help, and re-dedicating her life to God, her life was back on track and I began to see a woman of faith and courage live again. She had defeated depression and the spirit of suicide.

However, I found myself sinking into a deep pit of depression myself, and by the age of 18, I'd made my 1st suicide attempt. In June of 1994, after high school graduation, I was hopeless, despaired, and broken. I didn't want to live, and wondered what it felt like to have a happy life. Happy one second and crying the next, I had refused to keep living this way—ready to end it all. I recall crying and looking in the mirror being tormented by thoughts like: "you're ugly", and "you're dumb", "you're worthless", "you have no purpose to live", and "just kill yourself." After taking several anti-depression pills (overdosing), hoping I would go to sleep and not wake up, I was overtaken by an anointing like I had never experienced before ... Yes, it was God's love! I began to hear a sweet, quite spirit saying to me, "Theresa, don't kill yourself, I (Your God) loves you and have a purpose for your life. You will affect people by the millions, especially women!" I also heard Him say, "You know from experience how it feels to be broken, but what's broken? I, God, can put all things back together again." God saved my life that day and until present and all the days of my life, my soul says, yes.

Again in 2008 and 2010, I will never forget. I thought I had overcome depression in my young adult life; married, two beautiful children, a successful business owner and working in ministry, yet still suffering in silence. In 2008, I found myself struggling and battling more episodes of emotional breakdown. I regressed and came under such an attack of the enemy. The fear tried to overtake my life. Again, the enemy tried to convince me to give up (mind, body, and spirit). I was so afraid that I would lose my mind and end up in a mental institution. The more I entertained depression, the stronger the attack became... I was at my lowest, discouraged and in despair. My health was failing-to the point of death. I began to see all types of doctors. I was hospitalized twice. I began to have short-term memory loss, stopped eating, could not sleep, can't explain it, but it was awful. I was admitted in the wing of the psychiatric hospital for several days. I had no window, no visitors, no TV, nothing, but I had God.

Just like cancer and heart disease, mental illness can kill you. It was sucking the life out of me, but God is a present help in the time of trouble. While I was in the hospital, God had reminded me again about the lives that I will impact, and that day, I decided enough was enough. As I laid in the hospital, God spoke with authority to me and I heard Him say, "Listen to me and not the devil. I have a purpose for your life. Your life doesn't belong to you; your life is for my glory."

I fought with everything in me but a couple of years later, in the Spring of 2010, the battles became a war and I was beyond lost. I had hit rock bottom and could not pretend any longer. I was praying, trusting God's word but I never knew it would come back again. I thought the battle was over. After months of depression and oppression, spiritual bondage, and nightly battles with torment, I ended up in a parking lot attempting my second suicide attempt, sitting in my car, the last person I desired to talk too was my mom. I called my mom crying, and telling her how sorry I was but that I couldn't take anymore, and she screamed, "Theresa, where is your faith? I replied, "Mom, I am tired of that faith" stuff. I've been dealing with this battle over 20 years and I haven't won yet. I am tired spiritually, mentally, and physically. I just want you to take care of my children. I love you mom." My mom screamed, "No, please don't Theresa. Do you remember when I overdosed?

I too wanted to die but I decided to keep fighting because of you and your siblings. Please whatever you do, please live for your children." I then hung up the phone and decided to go get a facial, while I was getting the facial, the cool water mist began to blow over my face and tears began to roll down my face and I finally heard God whisper (I felt in my most darkest day he wasn't there) and finally after months, I felt his presence. He said I know you are tired but please go one more round and this time you will defeat the war of depression. I decided to go home and cry out to God.

I was admitted into the hospital for a second time but this time, I decided that enough was enough. As I laid in the hospital, God spoke with authority to me and I heard Him say, "Call unto me and I will answer thee, and show you great and mighty things you knowest not. (Jeremiah 33:3). I have a purpose for your life. Your life doesn't belong to you: your life is for my glory." After crying out to God, He instructed me to speak His word and I would receive instructions for healing and deliverance. I began to speak God's Word over my life with everything in me. "For God hath not given me the spirit of fear, but of power, of love and of a sound mind." 2 Timothy 1:7.

In the midst of the storm, I used the sword of the spirit, which is God's Word to defeat every attack of the enemy. This did not happen overnight; but one baby step after the next, I walked out of the attack. Every day, I became a little stronger and finally, I looked back and I was out. Lord, I thank you, and now I know that battle doesn't belong to me, it belongs to God. I renewed my mind with God's word and became victorious. I am even going through right now, I am still standing on the promises of God. He has kept me thus far, and I know He will continue to keep me in the midst of my trials. He wants me to tell you to stand on His word; He, God that promised, is faithful. So, if you don't know that God is still saving lives, still healing, still delivering, and still working miracles, then take a look at me. I am a living testimony! I received my healing and I am now walking in divine purpose with authority and boldness!

Are you feeling lost, depressed, broken or struggling with something?

If yes, God wanted me to share my struggle with you, it exposed my own battles, and the techniques which helped me to overcome them and what I learned from the experience. All of us are facing, will face, and in some cases, are still facing trials and tribulations. Through the power of God's grace and mercy, I have victoriously overcome the struggle of my past. Get ready to be inspired to pursue personal greatness and you too, will step into greatness. Get ready to chew on these delicious nuggets; I am about to share 31 pieces of my "Greater" nuggets to help you grow in the area of greatness for the mind, body, and spirit.

Taste and see that the LORD is good;
blessed is the one who takes refuge in Him.

—PSALM 34:8 (NIV)

1 PIECE NUGGET

Are you Ready to Say "Yes" to God?

And thou shalt love the Lord thy God with all thine heart, and with all thy soul, and with all thy mind.

–Deuteronomy 6:5 (KJV)

According to the Oxford Dictionaries, ALL is referred to the whole quantity or extent of a particular group or thing.

God wants you to give him a "yes" no matter what your situation presents. I am reminded that the whole duty of man is to fear and serve God. (Ecclesiastes 12:13) God created us to live a life that is pleasing in His sight, and has ordained us to fulfill a certain purpose. Conversely, the enemy wants to steal your "Yes", he wants to perplex the mind and the heart. I surrendered my life at the age of 18, and I am presently 40. Sometimes, I didn't feel like responding "Yes" especially when the trials and tribulations seemed to be unbearable. Today, I encourage you to surrender your all to God, just like when the police capture a criminal; he throws his hand up and surrenders under the authority of law enforcement. Today, throw your hands up and surrender your all to God, surrender your heart, mind, and soul. I can attest that this is the first step to living the abundant life that God has already predestined. Keep looking unto Jesus, the author, and finisher of our faith. Let's digest this nugget for a moment, and let's evaluate ourselves.

Are you giving God your best? Yes or No

_____

What is hindering you from giving God your all?

_____

_____

_____

Write a list of what's holding you back.

_____

_____

_____

_____

Now, Let it Go and Give it to God

Let's Pray

Lord, I have done everything that I can do. Today God, I ask that you step in and do what I can't do. God, I pray that you change me on the inside for only the pure in heart shall see you. I want a spirit to love and to please you no matter what comes or goes.

You made me and you know even the exact number of hairs on my head. Help me to surrender my mind, heart, and soul unto you. Ignite a fire within me to do your will and not my will. I give you permission to be the author and finisher of my faith.

I let go of anything that is holding me back, and I surrender to you my "All" from this day forward. Help me to forget those things which are behind, and reaching forth unto those things which are before me, according to your word and will.

IN JESUS NAME, AMEN.

Nugget Notes

2 PIECE NUGGETS

Write and Wait

Then the LORD answered me and said:
"Write the vision and make it plain on tablets,
that he may run who reads it.
For the vision is yet for an appointed time;"

–HABAKKUK 2:2-3 (NKJV)

What do you dream of?

Do you dream of starting a business?

Do you dream of writing a book?

Do you dream of being debt free?

Do you dream of losing weight?

What are you passionate about?

I remember reading this quote in Paula White's book which said *"I believe God is calling your destined state and not your present state. He has the ability to see you as you are to become."* Whatever your dream is, I encourage you to start writing it down with a date. Keep believing and keep waiting until you see the manifestation of what you wrote. We wait on the birth of a new baby. We wait in line at the grocery store. We wait to see the doctor or dentist. The Lord is teaching us that we must wait, and depend on Him. Learn to wait patiently because that is a part of learning to trust God. Here are examples of people that waited in the Bible:

- David waited (13 years) before he became King of Israel

- Abraham waited (25 years) for the birth of his son, Isaac

- Noah waited (120 years) from the time God told him to build the ark until the flood happened

- Man at the pool of Bethesda had an infirmity for (38 years) but he still had hope of being healed. He waited for the opportunity to step in the water and receive his healing

- _____ (Your name) has to wait on God!

Ok … your turn. I challenge you to keep a daily journal and write the vision, and at the appointed time God shall bring it to pass! Write, wait, but while you are waiting, ensure you work the vision, because faith without work is dead.

Start here

_____

_____

_____

_____

_____

_____

_____

_____

_____

_____

_____

_____

Challenge

Every day, I want you to allocate time to work on the vision that God has given you and don't allow the enemy to abort your vision.

Nugget Notes

_____

_____

_____

_____

_____

_____

_____

_____

_____

_____

_____

_____

_____

_____

_____

_____

_____

_____

_____

It Shall Come to PASS!

*For I am the LORD: I will speak, and the word that
I **shall** speak shall come to pass; it shall be no more
prolonged: for in your days, O rebellious house, will I
say the word, and will perform it, saith the Lord GOD.*

—EZEKIEL 12:25 (KJV)

Let's digest for a second, according to Oxford Dictionaries, "shall" means expressing a strong assertion or intention.

The word "shall" is mentioned 9,838 times in the Bible. If God said "SHALL" then it did happen. I want to challenge you that whatever your "it" is, start declaring and decreeing that 'it shall' come to pass according to the word of God.

According to 2 Corinthians 1:20, "for all the promises of God in Him are yea, and Amen, unto the glory of God by us." You are the child of the Most High God and you are entitled to His benefit!

My "shall" list:
Business – "It Shall Come to Pass!"
Ministry – "It Shall Come to Pass!"
Healing – "It Shall Come to Pass!"
Deliverance – "It Shall Come to Pass!"
Prosperity – "It Shall Come to Pass!"
Greatness – "It Shall Come to Pass!"

Write, your "shall" list

_____

_____

_____

_____

_____

_____

This nugget is so good, that I decided to give you an extra one for today. I know you hunger for more. Taste this one too, "Believe in the Lord your God, so shall ye be established and blessed; believe His prophets, and so shall ye prosper." 2 Chronicles 20:20 (KJV). You should be full now, so let's pray.

Let's Pray

Lord, I thank you for being a God of your word. You promised in your word that if I commit to you and trust you, that my plans "shall" succeed.

Help me to trust you and bind up the spirit of unbelief. I thank you in advance for you will bring my prayer request to pass according to your word and your will.

IN JESUS NAME, AMEN.

ONLY BELIEVE

Nugget Notes

_____

_____

_____

_____

_____

_____

_____

_____

_____

_____

_____

_____

_____

_____

_____

_____

_____

_____

4 PIECE NUGGETS

Don't Back Off!

Therefore my beloved brethren, be steadfast, unmovable, always abounding in the work of the Lord, for as ye know that your labor is not in vain in the Lord.

–1 Corinthians 15:58 (KJV)

Have you ever seen a dog that barked and stood its ground?

I recall approaching a dog, and the dog was barking, growling and showing its teeth. I remember thinking to myself that if I got any closer that this dog was going to attack or kill me; and by the way, it was a Rottweiler dog. The dog tried to intimidate me with his loud bark and keen teeth, but I was determined to enter the house to receive a gift (blessing) from a friend.

This is exactly what the enemy does, he wants you to quit. He wants you to faint. He wants to appear that he is bad, but face the enemy head on and let him know that with God, you are the baddest. Stand on the word of God, stand your ground and don't back off. Be steadfast ... Be unmovable and don't forget to put on the full armor of God. Stand firm with the *belt of truth* buckled around your waist, with *the breastplate of righteousness* in place, *your feet fitted with the readiness* (shoes) that comes from the gospel of peace and in addition to all of these, take up the *shield of faith*, with which you can extinguish all the flaming arrows of the evil one and take the *helmet of salvation* and the *sword of the Spirit*, which is the word of God. (Ephesians 6:10-18 NIV).

Challenge

Everyday encourage yourself in the Lord. I am more than a conqueror and this battle don't belong to me it belongs to the Lord!

Now, we are equipped and ready for

VICTORY!

Nugget Notes

_____

_____

_____

_____

_____

_____

_____

_____

_____

_____

_____

_____

_____

_____

_____

_____

_____

_____

_____

5 PIECE NUGGETS

Seek 1st

Seek you first the kingdom of God
and His righteousness;
and all these things shall be added unto you.

—Matthew 6:33 (KJV)

What kind of order is your life in?

In my salvation with Christ, I learned that I tend to get out of order. Every time I put others and things before God, He will send trials and tribulations to get my attention. In order to experience greatness in your life, you always need to put God 1st in everything, each and every day. If we truly seek Him first, which means to go in search or quest of Him, the Lord will bless you. Yet, society has conditioned you to seek a job, family, house and a car and so on. According to the scripture above, you have to seek God 1st. I heard a preacher say, "If you take care of God's business, then he will take care of your business." I challenge you today to strive daily to seek God 1st, start each morning with prayer and devotion to God.

I challenge you to seek God first every day!

GOD 1ST

MONDAY,

TUESDAY

WEDNESDAY

THURSDAY

FRIDAY

SATURDAY

SUNDAY

+

THE OTHER THINGS WILL
BE AUTOMATICALLY ADDED

Let's Pray

Lord, please forgive me if I've been putting other things first. Give me a mind and a heart to seek you early in the morning, every day! God, I always want to put you first in everything that I do. I know that if I seek you first with my whole heart, that I shall be rewarded as you have promised those who diligently seek you.

IN JESUS NAME, AMEN.

Nugget Notes

_____

_____

_____

_____

_____

_____

_____

_____

_____

_____

_____

_____

_____

_____

_____

_____

_____

_____

6 PIECE NUGGETS

In God "I" Trust

Put not your trust in princes, nor in the son of man, in whom there is no help.

—Psalm 146:3 (KJV)

Who do you trust in today?

In my life, I will admit that I have put trust in people and not totally in God. I learned that when I put my trust in man, I often was disappointed. Have you ever put your trust in someone, and they let you down. It's a hurtful feeling, and that hurtful feeling can lead to unforgiveness or hurt. Psalm 146:3 clearly states "that is better to take refuge in the Lord than to trust in man." Who are you putting your trust in today? Are you putting your trust in your doctor? Are you putting your trust in your spouse? Are you putting your trust in your lawyer? Are you putting your trust in the government system? Are you putting your trust in your job? I want to encourage you to put (100%) of your trust in God! God wants us to put all of our trust in Him, and when you trust Him, I promise, He will not fail you. Not only will God not fail you, but you will live a life of peace. When I decided to stop trusting so much in people and myself, I began to experience a life of peace and not turmoil. I want you to get in the habit of trusting God.

Let's affirm this every day:

Lord, I AM trusting in you!

Write down the things that you are trusting God to do for you

_____

_____

_____

_____

_____

_____

_____

_____

Let's pray

God, please forgive me if I have put my trust in man and help me to totally trust in you. I cast all my cares upon you for you care for me and you promised in your word that all things, whatsoever ye shall ask in prayer, believing, and ye shall receive.

Lord, I trust that you will answer my prayer according to your word and will.

IN JESUS NAME, AMEN.

Nugget Notes

7 PIECE NUGGETS

Brand New

*Forget the former things; **do not dwell** on the past.*
See, I am doing a new thing!

–Isaiah 43:18, 19 (NIV)

here's something about something being new!
I love the smell of new cars and when I wear new clothes, I feel great! When something is new, the excitement is just unexplainable! In order to experience greatness in your life, you have to think brand "new". The children of Israel were stubborn and had an "Egypt bondage" way of thinking. They were stuck in the past and as a result, they were kept from obtaining their promised future!

I want to challenge you today, to change the way you think! Pray that God will give you a brand new way of thinking! You can start right now! Why? Because today is a new day!

Are you wondering why you seem to be stuck? You know how it is … stuck with the same problem, stuck in depression, stuck in a bad relationship or either stuck in negative thinking! I have great news today; God is ready to do a new thing, but first, you need to surrender to God and allow Him to rewrite your life story!! Stop allowing the enemy to use your past to stop or delay your new beginnings. Pray that God will give you a new heart, maybe the heart you have now has hurt, pain, grief, disappointments, or even rejection inside!

I can attest that God will give you a new heart, a new way of thinking, a new way of talking and a new way of living!!! Let go of yesterday, and embrace this moment because God is doing a new thing!!!

Challenge

I challenge you to renew your mind daily by studying the word of God! I want you to start using this scripture to test what are you thinking about, and apply it to your life and you will begin to experience greatness in your mind, body, and spirit.

Philippians 4:8

- Whatsoever things are true
- Whatsoever things are honest
- Whatsoever things are just
- Whatsoever things are pure
- Whatsoever things are lovely
- Whatsoever things are of good report

If there be any virtue, and if there be any praise, think on these THINGS.

Nugget Notes

_____

_____

_____

_____

_____

_____

_____

_____

_____

_____

_____

_____

_____

_____

_____

_____

_____

DREAM
ASPIRING
CONVICTION
UNSTOPPABLE
BELIEVE
HARMONY
LOVE
BLISS
UNMOVABLE
CONVICTION
IMAGINE
UNSTOPPABLE
GIVE
THINK
RELIANCE
JOY
WISH
IMMORTAL
HONEST
UNDYING
HEALING
JOY
BLESSING
THINK
IMAGINE
UNMOVABLE
HOPE
PROSPERITY
TRUST
IMMORTAL
LOVE
HELP
JOY
GIVE
LOVE
BLISS
DREAM
PEACE
HOPE
UNSTOPPABLE
SPIRIT
HEALING
HOPE
UNDYING
CALM
WISH
SPIRIT
BLISS
JOY
CALM
BLESSING
CALM
TRUST
PEACE
BELIEVE
WORSHIP
DELIGHT
HELP
JOY
HEALING
RELIANCE
PROSPERITY
LIFE
IT'S POSSIBLE
L O V E
D R E A M

8 PIECE NUGGETS

I am a Winner!

Blessed is the man that endureth temptation:
for when he is tried, he shall receive the crown of life,
which the Lord hath promised to them that love him.

–JAMES 1:12 (KJV)

What do you want to win?
Let me answer this for you; you want to win the crown of life (enteral life)!! The enemy's job is to keep you from winning the crown of life. The thief comes only to steal and kill and destroy: I have come that they may have life, and have it to the full. (John 10:10) He tends to bring distraction to keep you from focusing on winning your crown of life. I don't know anything about the Super Bowl, but I do know SUPER Jesus! With Him, you can win every game. Keep enduring temptation. Keep enduring trials and tribulation. Remember, if you can endure, the Lord has promised you a great reward!

Let's Pray

God, please give me the strength to endure hardship as a good solider. Sometimes, I feel a little weak, but help me to know when I can't, that you can, God. Help me to stay focused on the main goal which is the crown of life. God, bind up every attack from the enemy, and forgive me for any thinking that wasn't pleasing in your sight. I thank you.

IN JESUS NAME, AMEN.

Nugget Notes

_____

_____

_____

_____

_____

_____

_____

_____

_____

_____

_____

_____

_____

_____

_____

_____

_____

9 PIECE NUGGETS

He is On Your Side

What then shall we say to these things?
If God is for us, who can be against us?

—Romans 8:31 (KJV)

Do you feel like you are walking in your purpose? Most people are not walking in their fullest potential. I struggled for a long time with my purpose. I looked for approval from other people, especially close friends and family members. I had to learn not to seek the approval of others. You see, when you were born, God had already placed a gift or talent within you, but it's your responsibility to utilize what He has given unto you. When I decided to stop seeking people's approval, I began to feel like I was finally walking in my purpose for life. I am happier than ever.

It's time to stop getting people's approval. It's time to stop getting people's opinion. It's time to discharge dream killers! Have you ever asked someone about starting a business, and they replied you don't have a degree or resources. Guess what? Most people would stop right there because of the opinion of others. Whatever God is tugging at you to do, just do it … God promised that if He is for you that nothing can be against you. God is on your side, you have everything you need.

Challenge

Stop being influenced by the opinions of other people. You don't need their approval.

GOD IS ON YOUR SIDE

Nugget Notes

10 PIECE NUGGETS

Pass the Test for the Testimony

*That the trial of your faith, being much more
precious than of gold that perisheth, though it be
tried with fire, might be found unto praise and
honor and glory at the appearing of Jesus Christ.*

–1 Peter 1:7 (KJV)

I've been on this walk with God for over 20 years and I am not going to say every day is going to be easy. As I matured in my faith, my tests allowed me to mature in my Christian walk. I remember when I was first saved and had gotten sick. God wanted me to trust that He could heal a headache. Years later, I was diagnosed with major health issues that affected my memory and my nervous system to the point that I could barely walk and hold items in my hands. I had to trust God for that too. It's just like starting preschool; you learn alphabet and numbers and once you have retained and passed that information, you are promoted to the next level. Don't you think that it would be very strange for a college student to be learning their alphabets? God wants us to pass the tests and mature in our walk with faith and power. If you keep failing the test, you will remain in that same trial until God has perfected that area.

My trails and tests have allowed me to testify. Testimonies are not for you, but to make known God's good deeds to others and to increase your faith.

Let me share a few of my testimonies:

- I know God as a provider; I lost everything and went bankrupt!

- I know God as a comforter; I lost my mom!

- I know God as a mender of a broken heart; I was abused both physically and emotionally!

- I know God as a miracle worker; the doctor said I couldn't have children, I have two!

- I know God as a teacher; I was writing on a 3rd grade level as a freshman in college and now I have written my first book!

What are some of your testimonies? Write them below. Thank God and now share your testimony with others.

_____

_____

_____

_____

_____

_____

_____

_____

Sometimes, it is good to reflect on what God has already done, and if God brought you through that, then he can bring you out of your current trial or tribulation. God is the same yesterday, today, and forevermore.

I am going to pass this test, because it will become my testimony!

Nugget Notes

_____

_____

_____

_____

_____

_____

_____

_____

_____

_____

_____

_____

_____

_____

_____

_____

_____

_____

11 PIECE NUGGETS

Exceedingly, Abundantly, and Above

Now unto him that is able to do exceedingly,
abundantly above all that we ask or think,
according to the power that worketh in us.

—Ephesians 3:20 (KJV)

*L*et's define a few words.

First, according to Oxford Dictionaries, exceedingly means very great, abundantly means plentifully, and above means at a higher level.

Wow, that's a lot.

Are you expecting little? God is a God of the highest degree. Our minds can't comprehend how big our God is; it would just explode. Whatever we ask, God is able to do it, plentifully and at a higher level, but it's according to the power that worketh in you. Trust God to give you more than enough. I began to apply the word of God to my finances, I never settled for a limited amount of income, every year, God has increased my income, more and more every year!! I'm reminded of the story of how Peter toiled all night for fishes and caught nothing, but Jesus approached him and told the professional fisherman to launch out into the deep, and he obeyed Jesus. Peter had so many fishes that the net broke! I want to encourage you today to take the limit off God and allow God to be an EXCEEDINGLY, ABUDANTLY, AND ABOVE GOD!

Journal

Write a "big" prayer request and trust God that He will do more than what you expect!

_____

_____

_____

_____

_____

_____

_____

_____

_____

_____

Let's Pray

Lord, I take the limit off you. I know that you are a big God and help me to trust you to do big things in my life. God bless me with an overflow that I will be able to help others. I pray for overflow of love, joy, peace, and prosperity. I thank you for the more than enough blessings in my life.

IN JESUS NAME, AMEN.

GOD
IS BIG!

Nugget Notes

12 PIECE NUGGETS

Wonderfully Made

I will praise you, for I am fearfully and wonderfully made, marvelous are your works and that my soul knows very well.

—Psalm 139:14 (NKJV)

Ok. Think about yourself for a second … What did you just think about yourself? Did you think that you were?

Ugly or Pretty?

Smart or Dumb?

Fat or Skinny?

Worthy or Worthless?

Spring 1994, at the age of 18 (senior in high school) and the year God saved my life. I struggled with self-identity, not knowing who I was, but what others told me I was. Starting at the age of 5 years old, I was assaulted with someone's words, taunted and teased at school. I had speech impairment, and the children would tell me to say a specific word and laugh. Do you remember the children's song about sticks and stones? It's not true…In fact; words can break our hearts and can actually stop us from fulfilling our destinies. I suffered from emotional abuse. I had that loved one that told me I was dumb. I had that boy that I really liked told me I was ugly. I had relationships with people that were very controlling and domineering, whatever they said, I did. Then in middle school, I had a severe case of chickenpox which left spots on my face. So, even when I looked in the mirror, I thought I was ugly. I had a learning disorder, and I believed I was dumb. Not only did I believe that I was dumb, but I also believed that I was worthless and because of the enemy, I wrestled with those thoughts which left me with a sense of hopelessness. I can attest that I am no longer feeling those negative thoughts. I had to (and still to this day) renew my mind with the word of God. I decided that enough was enough. I started cutting those defeated words with the sword of the spirit, which is God's word to defeat every thought by the attack of the enemy. I am beautiful. I am worthy.

I want to let you know that you are wonderfully made by God, and to encourage you to be thankful of how God made you. God loves you and you can't truly love others if you don't love yourself.

It's your turn, please journal 10 attributes you love about yourself and then thank God.

1.

2.

3.

4.

5.

6.

7.

8.

9.

10.

Let's Pray

God, I want to ask you to forgive me for the thoughts that I think which are not pleasing to you. I thank you for creating me, because you said that I am fearfully and wonderfully made. Please heal me from any bad thoughts that I have experienced in the past or where others have spoken over my life. Help me to renew my thoughts daily in your word. God help me to move in the area of greatness in my mind, because you did promise in your word that whatsoever a man thinks, so is he.

IN JESUS NAME, AMEN.

Nugget Notes

_____

_____

_____

_____

_____

_____

_____

_____

_____

_____

_____

_____

_____

_____

_____

_____

_____

13 PIECE NUGGETS

My Name Is

For to us a child is born, to us a son is given,
and the government will be on his shoulders.
And he will be called, Wonderful Counselor,
Mighty God, Everlasting Father, Prince of Peace

—Isaiah 9:6 New International Version (NIV)

Everyone has a name, and sometimes, a nickname. In my walk with Christ, I can attest that whatever you need is in the name of Jesus. I got healing in that name. I got deliverance in that name. I got saved in that name. I got blessed in that name. I got joy in that name. I got peace in that name. The list goes on and on! Whatever you need for that specific situation that you might be experiencing, call Him by that name.

Let me share just a few of God's names that I found on www.smilegodlovesyour.org:

- Elohim: A reference to God's power and might
- Jehovah-Rohi: The Lord is my shepherd

- Jehovah-Jireh: The Lord will provide
- I Am
- King
- Lord God Almighty
- Creator

- Everlasting Father
- Guide
- OMEGA
- Potter
- Prince of Peace
- Teacher

You see, whatever you need is all in the name of Jesus!!! Call Him by His name, and I promise He will answer.

Reflection Moment

What "name" do I need today? Meditate on that name and search a scripture and trust God for whatever you need him to be today.

_____

_____

_____

_____

MMMMM … This is getting good!

I decided to add extra meat to the following nuggets, which is more of the word of God! So, get ready and let your soul delight itself in fatness!

Nugget Notes

14 PIECE NUGGETS

I am Your Hiding Place

You are my hiding place; you will protect me from trouble and surround me with songs of deliverance.

–Psalms 32:7 (NIV)

A child is never more confident than when he is in his/her father's arms. To him/her, the father is a superman, no matter how frail the father might be in reality. When threatened by bullies or there is a rampage, he/she runs into those arms, looks up to the father and trusts his judgment, believing that he is up to any task.

The hiding place of the most High and the shadow of the Almighty offers a more surer ground of confidence for a child of God, by this I mean one who has identified with Christ and the cross. It (hiding place of the most High) serves as the best place, second to none any mortal father can provide. The hiding place of the Most High is not a physical hemisphere neither is it a place built by hands. It is a spiritual atmosphere in which the faith and life of a believer is in line with God's righteousness thereby drawing down His presence and power for deliverance in times of trouble. It is a life of intimate relationship and communion with God with full assurance of divine protection and deliverance on every side. Only those who dwell under the secret place of the Most High can abide under the shadow of the Almighty.

There can be no better place to be in this troublous world. Dwellers of this hiding place are hereby promised peculiar and comprehensive packages of blessings. The blessings include: protection, preservation, privileges, provision, power, promotion and permanence (longevity).

Four (4) things God is to those in His hiding place and under His shadow;

1 A refuge

2 A fortress

3 God, a true and faithful God

4 A trust, a place of security

Now, let's hide in the secret place of the Most High God!

Let's pray

Jesus, since one in sin cannot be in your hiding place, I sincerely confess my sins today, that I may experience your presence and power and be a resident in your hiding place.

IN JESUS NAME, AMEN.

Nugget Notes

DREAM ASPIRING CONVICTION UNSTOPPABLE BELIEVE HARMONY LOVE BLISS UNMOVABLE CONVICTION IMAGINE UNSTOPPABLE GIVE THINK RELIANCE
JOY WISH IMMORTAL HONEST IMMORTAL
UNDYING JOY HEALING HOPE PROSPERITY TRUST
LOVE HELP BLESSING THINK IMAGINE UNMOVABLE DREAM PEACE
JOY GIVE LOVE BLISS
HOPE
UNSTOPPABLE HEALING
CALM BLESSING SPIRIT CALM HOPE UNDYING CALM WISH SPIRIT BLISS
JOY PEACE BELIEVE WORSHIP DELIGHT TRUST
HEALING RELIANCE HELP JOY
PROSPERITY LIFE IT'S POSSIBLE LOVE DREAM

15 PIECE NUGGETS

Non-Void

So shall my word be that goeth forth
out of my mouth: it shall not return unto me void,
but it shall accomplish that which I please,
and it shall prosper in the thing where to I sent it.

—Isaiah 55:11 (KJV)

According to Dictonary.com, void is defined as having no legal force or effect.

Have you ever received a check and noticed in the corner that after 180 days or more, the bank did not have to honor that check. Do you know that when God's word goes out, it will not return to Him void no matter how long it takes? The word of God was spoken and it shall be made good. So, don't give up so quickly, know that if God said it, it shall come to pass. What word has God spoken to you?

Write down a few scriptures relevant to your situation or circumstance.

_____

_____

_____

_____

_____

_____

_____

I challenge you to speak the word of God and trust that His Words will not return to Him void.

God's word will not return unto him void!

Nugget Notes

16 PIECE NUGGETS

Rise Above

So shall they fear the name of the Lord from the west,
and is glory from the rising of the sun.
When the enemy shall come in like a flood, the spirit
of the Lord shall lift up a standard against him.

—Isaiah 59:19 (KJV)

Many a times in life, we face adverse challenges. Many of which we lose hope and courage, we tend to question God about the way life has been treating us. I do ask myself a question; is life fair? Why will after trusting God, we still find ourselves in the pit of life? It seems God is far from us and our prayers seem unanswered. Some of life challenges threaten our hope and our heart begins to ponder on questioning the existence of God. Circumstances have beaten us both within and without and we hide within caves to survive.

Hear this good news, your redeemer lives, you might be looking at the state of your health, not enough money to pay your bills, economy recession and enemies you may picture fighting against your soul. Remember, no matter what, God will raise a standard against your enemies and you will rise above them all. Stop looking at those challenges, look up to Jesus; the author and finisher of our faith for we do not walk by sight but by faith. We must therefore, walk in the reality of the finished work of Christ, because all heart stony issues and problems are finished on the cross and we are seated with Christ in the heavenly places far above principalities and powers.

Let's pray

Lord, help me to look up to you always and understand that all things are working together for my good.

Rise above that pain!
Rise above that past!
Rise above that adversity!
Rise above that sickness!
Rise above that depression!
Rise above that loneliness!
Rise above that grief!
Rise above that setback!
Rise above that failure!
Rise above that mistake!

Now you say it:
I will rise above All!

Nugget Notes

17 PIECE NUGGETS

Extra Strength

I can do all things through Christ that strengthens me.

–PHILIPPIANS 4:13 (KJV)

here is a limit to the strength in a man because we live in a physical realm. So to enjoy the supernatural strength, we need to acknowledge the source, author and giver of strength. So many people get frustrated on the pathway to destiny, they get wearied. Let me tell you a simple story from the bible in the book of *Samuel 30:1.*

That David returned to Ziklag and the Amalekites invaded the south and Ziklag was smitten, burnt with fire and the whole city was taken captive. David and his men just arrived from a war front and they were exhausted, the whole warriors were lamenting because their families were taken captives and homeless.

They needed extra strength and to win but David trusted the Lord and went with his soldiers and they took back what the enemies had taken from them, they defeated the Amalekites and killed them, from night to morning. They recorded exceptional victory even when there was no strength in them, because they acknowledge the author of strength.

Maybe today you are running out of strength? All you need is to acknowledge Jesus and He will give you strength to rise above every obstacles and hindrances. We must understand that by strength shall no man prevail and you can't go far with the little strength of your own. We need to arise and be strengthened with might in the inner man to face our fears with His strength.

Let's pray

Father, I need your strength to rise above obstacles and challenges. I acknowledge you as the source of strength to fulfill my destiny amidst every mountain of life.

In Jesus Name, Amen.

Let the weak say, I AM STRONG!

–Joel 3:10 (NIV)

Nugget Notes

18 PIECE NUGGETS

It's Time to Cross Over

Now when he had left speaking,
he said unto Simon,
"Launch out into the deep,
and let down your nets for a draught."

–Luke 5:4 (KJV)

*E*veryone loves to cross over to a better side of life. The Israelites were on servitude for four hundred and thirty years, and they hoped for a cross over one day until God appointed Moses on their behalf. (Exodus 12:4) The appearing day for their crossing over was the best moment for the Israelites to this today. Are you stressed out of life, working tremendously with low income but high debt, experiencing lack of finance, does your business seem to be failing? Remember, Peter toiled all night and the best time for fishing is at night. Even though the five realities of fishing were put in place;

- Peter was a professional fisherman
- Peter went out with professionally perfect fishermen
- Peter went out with the best equipment
- He went at the right time
- He went to the best position

Yet, life forced him to knee in frustration. But Jesus came over that morning after a great night of toiling without a single fish in their boat, though the atmosphere was not conducive for fishing, but there was a great harvest that day because Jesus had come to put an end to their toiling throughout the night.

Let me assure you at this very moment that Jesus is coming into your boat and you are crossing every obstacles and hindrances. For your time of rejoicing has come, no more hindrance, no more losses. Your boat is about to overflow, are you ready?

Let's pray

Father, come into my boat and sail over to the better side of life. I decree that I am crossing over every obstacle of my life.

IN JESUS NAME, AMEN.

Nugget Notes

19 PIECE NUGGETS

Mighty to Save

If be so, our God whom we serve is able
to deliver us from the burning fiery furnace,
and He will deliver us out of thine hand, O king.

–Daniel 3:17 (KJV)

*M*any times, we are caught up in the web of challenges and troubles, victimized when we are innocent, abused by a well-respected person, lose all we could call ours, life becomes tough and meaningless and it seems as if the whole world is crumbling down on us. We lose hope and tend to give it all up regretting our existence on earth, but the Lord is saying to you today that He is close; He can see your troubles, He is able to save, rescue you and give you a lively hope. The Lord is close to the broken hearted; He rescues those who are crushed in the spirit.

The LORD is closer and cares much more for you than what you think, see, feel or experience. His hands are not shortened that it cannot save; neither are His ears heavy that it cannot hear you from your troubles. (Is 59:1); but, one thing has been keeping Him from acting on our behalf.

What is this thing?

Ps.34:17; the LORD hears His people *when they call to Him for help.* He rescues them from all their troubles.

This passage describes God's ability to rescue His people with a conditional statement of when they call on Him for help. Since you've been going through this tough time, have you ever gone on your knees to pray and ask for God's help to deliver you? God is able to do exceedingly, abundantly above all that we ask or think, according to the power that works in us (Eph3:20) just as He delivered Shadrach, Meshach and Abednego from the fiery furnace of King Nebuchadnezzar, He delivered Peter from prison, He is also set to deliver you from all troubles, challenges, problems that have surrounded you. All you have to do is to call on Him. Join me today, as we ask for God's help together, in unity of the spirit. Call to me and I will answer you and show you great and mighty things which thou knowest not (Jer 33:3). This is a promise for those who expect comfort from the Lord.

What do you need God to save you from?

Challenge

Call on God to save you

_____

_____

_____

_____

_____

_____

_____

Let's Pray

Lord Jesus, I come boldly to the throne of grace today that I may obtain mercy and find grace to help me in the time of need. I lift up my eyes to you, Lord help me. I receive help and I am victorious.

IN JESUS NAME, AMEN.

Nugget Notes

20 PIECE NUGGETS

Special Order

Delight thyself also in the Lord;
and he shall give thee the desires of thine heart.
Commit thy way unto the Lord;
Trust also in him; and he shall bring it to pass.

—Psalm 37:4-5 (KJV)

Delight in the Lord
Commit in the Lord
Trust in the Lord
It shall come to pass!

Let's affirm this every day

I am, confident in my vision, committed to the work because God says; it should be according to his Word.

Nugget Notes

Draw Nigh to God

Draw nigh to God, and he will draw nigh to you. Cleanse your hands, ye sinners; and purify your heart, ye double minded.

–James 4:8 (KJV)

There is something about God that every Christian should know: God always waits for us to make a move, the first move before He moves to meet us. This is a fact of the word of God that we must come to reckon with.

I want us to look at the Old Testament passage that will help to bring out this truth some more. It is found in 2 Chronicles 15: 1-2 *"Now the Spirit of God came upon Azariah the son of Oded. And he went out to meet Asa, and said to him: "Hear me, Asa, and all Judah and Benjamin. The LORD is with you while you are with Him. If you seek Him, He will be found by you: but if you forsake Him, He will forsake you."*

You see, God is with you while you are with Him, if you seek and look for Him He will reveal Himself to you. And if we forsake Him, He will forsake us.

Let us draw near to God consciously and He will draw near to us. Seek God in repentance, in fasting and in prayers and true to His nature, He will show Himself to us.

We see in the life and ministry of Jesus, this same fact. He never goes hop scorching His power arbitrarily on people, He always waits for people to come to Him asking for His help. Even when He knows one sick or blind, He still asks the person what he wants Him to do for him.

God has not changed. If we want Him to do anything for us, we would need to come near to Him close enough to ask Him for it. He is waiting for you to make the first move.

Let's pray

Thank you God for the promise of your word that guarantees that if I seek you, I will find you, now I ask for grace to go all out for you in the name of Jesus. Amen.

Nugget Notes

_____

_____

_____

_____

_____

_____

_____

_____

_____

_____

_____

_____

_____

_____

_____

_____

_____

_____

_____

DREAM ASPIRING CONVICTION UNSTOPPABLE BELIEVE HARMONY LOVE BLISS UNSTOPPABLE GIVE THINK RELIANCE
JOY WISH IMMORTAL HONEST CONVICTION IMAGINE
LOVE UNDYING JOY HEALING HOPE UNMOVABLE IMMORTAL TRUST UNSTOPPABLE CONVICTION UNMOVABLE
HELP JOY GIVE LOVE BLISS THINK BLESSING IMAGINE SPIRIT PROSPERITY
HOPE PEACE DREAM
UNSTOPPABLE HEALING UNDYING CALM WISH SPIRIT BLISS
JOY CALM BLESSING HOPE HEALING
PEACE BELIEVE WORSHIP DELIGHT CALM TRUST
HEALING RELIANCE HELP JOY LOVE
PROSPERITY IT'S POSSIBLE DREAM

22 PIECE NUGGETS

Small Beginnings

Though thy beginning was small,
yet thy latter end should greatly increase.

–Job 8:7 (KJV)

The beginning of a thing is very important because it serves as the foundation upon which everything else stands. The way you begin a thing can determine the speed, attitude and the degree of success or failure you will experience in it.

From our grand knowledge of natural science, we understand how fetus is developed - from fertilization of eggs to embryo and to fetus. Every present president of a nation was once a fetus and gradually developed into a mighty man of influence and affluence. When I was a child, I spoke like a child, reasoned as a child and understood as a child. Many big businesses we see today have their foundation perfectly structured from their little beginning. There is always a beginning phase at every junction of life.

One challenge most believers face is the inability to reconcile Gods timing with theirs. We find it difficult to link our present to our future. One thing that may ring a bell in our heart daily is that God specializes in calling those things that were not as though they were; if He calls you a manager and you are presently serving as a messenger. Never despise the position that looks inconsequential. Never despise the location that looks unpromising, never despise that small marriage because that level you are now is not your destination; you are on a mission and you can never be through until the whole world has seen the glory of God in your life.

Despise not small beginnings

Let's pray

Father, I thank you for my current position and phase of life, I receive grace to move on no matter the opposition that I might face on my journey to greatness.

IN JESUS NAME, AMEN

Nugget Notes

23 PIECE NUGGETS

Shhhh, Listen to Me

He staggered not at the promise of God through
unbelief; but was strong in faith, giving glory to God;

–Romans 4:20 (KJV)

There are so many noises that distract us from what the Lord is saying. The influence of men on us has negated the word of God and made it of no effect in our lives.

Though there will be different obstacles fighting against every one of Gods promises for us and our environment gives us a picture of how impotent those promises are, after a series of waiting, these promises have not been fulfilled or seem delayed, we tend to compare ourselves to others who do not believe in these promises, but are flourishing outside the jurisdiction of His word. This has a great influence on our faith.

From our memory verse, the Lord told Abraham about His promises through naturally speaking. It seemed impossible for Abraham to give birth at that age. But the word of the Lord explained here that; Abraham staggered not at the promises of God. I know this sounds foolish and unbelievable to a mere man but He hath chosen the foolish things to confound the wise. So criticism came from friends and foes, but Abraham was strong in faith and continued giving glory to God.

I admonish you today to be patient and strong in faith for after a little while, the promises will be fulfilled. Faithful is He that promised and He will make it come to pass.

Let's pray

Lord my faith looks up to thee; strengthen me to wait a little longer and not to compromise my faith.

IN JESUS NAME, AMEN.

Nugget Notes

24 PIECE NUGGETS

You are Not Alone

*Be strong and of a good courage, fear not, nor be
afraid of them: for the LORD thy God, He is that doth
go with thee; He will not fail thee, nor forsake thee.*

–DEUTERONOMY 31:6 (KJV)

The word "fear not" appears 365 times in the bible,
which is pointing us to the fact that, each "fear not"
is attached to a day of the year. We live in a world of fear;
fear of losing in business, fear of broken marriages, fear of
insecurity within or without, political crisis, etc. all these
fuel our curiosity towards living a better life out there.
Some years back, I was scared about going into business
because of the parties involved, I was scared of their per-
sonalities thereby having a low class esteem of myself. But
I was inspired by this passage of the scripture emphasizing
the word "be strong and be of good courage, fear not, for
you are not alone". I knew I was least in this company of
people and their portfolio, but deep down within me, I

knew I was not alone. When we sat for the meeting and my business ordeal was approved, though being the least I was highly favored by courageously taking on my world with boldness to smile at my feet. My question to you this morning is; what are your fears? What are your worries? Why not cast all yours cares upon Him and be anxious for nothing and walk in this level of confidence?

Let's Pray

Father, give me the spirit of love, power and sound mind. Help me to realize you are always with me and not to live in fear. Help me to stand in the reality of who resides in me.

IN JESUS NAME, AMEN.

Nugget Notes

25 PIECE NUGGETS

Come out of the Grave

And when He thus had spoken, He cried with
a loud voice, "Lazarus, come forth".

–John 11:43 (KJV)

The grave is said to be a quiet disposition of unused talents and glory. Men who died without fully rising to their peak, men whose potentials were wasted, men who fall under this category are approximately 75%. I say to myself, there is a height yet to be reached and voices yet to be heard. When things were tough back then, I kept pressing my spirit with the right words, saying I will not die inside this pit of circumstances. The fact that you came from a poor background doesn't make your back to remain on the ground.

Our economy awaits saviors, and our nation is anticipating for the full manifestation of the sons of God, yet our potentials are left untouched and the silent grave calls for glory reserved, but I'm happy to announce to you today: it is time to break the chain of mediocrity, failure and ignorance of living lesser than what we are created to be. I come out of my grave for the world to see God glory upon me. It's time to come out the grave of depression. It's time to come out the grave or hopelessness.

Before you can come out of your grave, you will definitely need help. For Lazarus to come out of his grave, Jesus cried out with a loud voice – "A voice that brought that which was dead back to life." Lazarus who was hopeless now became the first apostle to fully manifest his potentials in Bethany. Finally, until you come out of the grave, you will die lesser than your mandate on earth, though ye are gods but you will die like mere men. Jesus is the only help needed to come out of this grave.

Let's Pray

Father, I cry out with a loud voice this hour, open my grave that I may live up to your expectations. Help me not to die with this instinct inside of me in your name (Jesus) I pray, Amen.

Nugget Notes

26 PIECE NUGGETS

Special Order

But someone will say,
"You have faith; I have deeds."
Show me your faith without deeds,
and I will show you my faith by my deeds.

—James 2:18 (NIV)

Let's affirm this every day

My opposition is an opportunity to witness/share my faith in ACTION.

Nugget Notes

27 PIECE NUGGETS

Special Order

God is not human, that he should lie,
not a human being,
that he should change his mind.
Does he speak and then not act?
Does he promise and not fulfill?

–Numbers 23:19 (NIV)

The word of God is the revealed truth.

Let's affirm this every day

I am equipped to face every challenge and succeed-excel in reaching the promise end.

Nugget Notes

28 PIECE NUGGETS

Heal My Heart

The LORD is near unto them that are of a broken heart; and saveth such as be of a contrite spirit.

–PSALM 34:18

$\mathcal{I}$ think everyone has had their heart broken at some critical junction of life. Mine was broken when I lost my mom, and it took me a very long time to get over it. The pain was indescribable. Some people say it's like having your heart dug out with a spoon. Some other person's broken heart might be due to a job loss, failed exam, bereavement, disappointment, rejection or ridicule. But I'm happy to announce to you that God cares. He's hurt with you. What was He doing when you were weeping? It will amaze you to know that He was weeping too. In fact, it is in your pain that God is closest to you, whether you realize it or not.

God says for the heart that's resentful, I'll give you a heart of peace. For the heart that's anxious, I'll give a heart that's confident. For a heart that is lonely, I'll give you a heart full of overflowing love. That heart that has been bitter and angry, I'll give a forgiving, loving and generous heart instead. All He's asking to do in your life is a heart transplant.

Why do we need freedom? Do we need a healing or touch? Because we are enslaved by the expectations of others, past memories, future fears, current pressures, opinions of society, and so on. But all you need is to open your heart to Jesus and give Him one hundred percent. Say, like David 'I run in the path of your commands, for you have set my heart free'.

Let's pray: Lord Jesus, I come to you today, believing and asking you for a healing upon my heart and I receive in faith.

IN JESUS NAME, AMEN.

Nugget Notes

29 PIECE NUGGETS

Restore & Recover

And I will restore to you the years that the locust hath
eaten, the cankerworm, and the caterpillar, and the
palmerworm, my great army which I sent among you

–JOEL 2:25

*M*oney can be restored, as well as property, relationships, etc. But one thing that can never be
restored is time. Time flies and it doesn't return. Years pass
and we never get them back. Yet, God promises the impossible "I will restore the years that the locust has eaten". The
immediate meaning of this promise is clear. God's people
had suffered a complete destruction of their entire harvest
through swarms of locusts that marched like an insect's
army through their land, destroying the crops. For four
consecutive years, their harvest was completely wiped out.

After restoring what was destroyed, the Lord goes on
to promise even more. Though Joel is speaking to a nation,
it's important to reflect on these promises from God on

a personal level. Not only are we as a society resurrected from sin because of Christ's sacrifice, we are corporately and individually given life in the Holy Ghost. In the midst of judgment, God shows His mercy. When we allow God to work in our lives, we give Him the access He needs to clean the locust (the invading enemy of our soul), destroy and build up what the Spirit delivers. The Holy Spirit, in effect, redeems what was lost by working through our lives.

Let's pray

Lord, I have spent too many years without you. Fill my heart with love and gratitude for Christ and let the loss of these years make my love for Christ greater than it has ever been.

IN JESUS NAME, AMEN.

Nugget Notes

Something Great is About to Happen

"Call to me and I will answer you and tell you great and unsearchable things you do not know"

–Jeremiah 33:3 (*NIV*)

*I*n ancient times, Israel was known to be the ruling people over the world, but due to their inability to see God, shrouded with their challenges and barriers, they conquered in the past, they became full of themselves to the point that a lesser country defeated Israel and their glory was trampled upon. Relating this to our lives as believers, our past success and the terrible circumstances faced have left us with a scar within our bones and we tend to give ourselves some consolation from past ashes. We trusted so much in the arms of flesh and our hope has been dashed, our daughters have been taken into slavery, our businesses have become desolate and we're lost in our pains and anguish. How can a King be walking bare footed and the Queen be tormented in her palace? But the voice of the Lord is coming to you this morning from His word that something great is about to happen only if we can call unto our God: in whose name there is nothing impossible.

Israelites were restored, after calling on God when the battle was deadly and their shame was turned to double honor and their glory shone like the sun again in Jerusalem.

I challenge you to take up your crutches and call unto the Lord for full restoration lest the enemy rejoice over your downfall. Your rising is dependent on your decision to call on Him.

Let's pray

Father, I refuse to glory in the past, I see you as Lord who is there to help in time of need. I call on you today, answer me speedily. Let my glory be restored today. Do a new thing in my Life oh Lord!!

IN JESUS NAME, AMEN.

Nugget Notes

Active to Overcome – Activating the Ability

The image of everything great is before you. Everything you could possibly conceive is within your grasp. The price to obtain it is your decision. How much are you willing to believe? Are you ready to invest in it?

Stepping beyond accepting the possibility. (?) Are you willing to trust the opportunity enough to put your plans into action?

In fact, the key to seeing the promise you envision is based upon your willingess to travel the road necessary to reach it. You have the power to see (imagine). The gift and the ability (to be) lives in your belief. Do you see yourself taking the next step? Can you envision the importance of a simple strategy? The particulars tend to vary. Yet it all begins with a step. The beautiful truth about the step is that it too is in you. An essential part of your character, in your developing faith (the trust and belief) is the strength and confidence to act. The challenge you face in achieving the point of promise is to keep a simple reminder that the

Word said! God ordained. God inspired. He allocated your power, your purpose, and your ability in His Word. But for you to step beyond yesterday's futile limit you need only the skill of remembering what it took to get you to where you are now. How did you reach this point? And what is it that you're promised? The giants, the obstacles, the limits; they aren't the promise. They are there perhaps to guard what's yours from any and all impostors and disbelievers.

Nugget Notes

_____

_____

_____

_____

_____

_____

_____

_____

_____

_____

_____

_____

_____

_____

_____

_____

_____

_____

DREAM
ASPIRING
CONVICTION
UNSTOPPABLE
BELIEVE
HARMONY
LOVE
BLISS
UNMOVABLE
CONVICTION
IMAGINE
UNSTOPPABLE
GIVE
THINK
RELIANCE
JOY
WISH
IMMORTAL
HONEST
UNDYING
HEALING
JOY
BLESSING
THINK
IMAGINE
UNMOVABLE
HOPE
PEACE
DREAM
PROSPERITY
TRUST
IMMORTAL
LOVE
HELP
HOPE
JOY
GIVE
LOVE
BLISS
UNSTOPPABLE
SPIRIT
HEALING
HOPE
UNDYING
TRUST
JOY
CALM
WISH
BLISS
SPIRIT
CALM
BLESSING
DELIGHT
RELIANCE
CALM
HELP
JOY
PEACE
BELIEVE
WORSHIP
HEALING
PROSPERITY
LIFE
IT'S POSSIBLE
LOVE
DREAM

Acknowledgements

I know right now you should be full and have gained some weight of greatness in your mind, body, and spirit. Don't you worry; a new batch of nuggets will be coming up soon. I do have to acknowledge the following, because without them, I could have never experienced my "greatness" in my personal life.

To the depression, thank you.

To the low self-esteem, thank you.

To the fear, thank you.

To the doubt, thank you.

To the rejection, thank you.

To the brokenness, thank you.

To the lack, thank you.

And definitely to the spirit of suicide, thank you.

Because I didn't allow you to drive me from my purpose, but to my greatness! My powerless, painful past is now my press through purpose. Remember, I see greatness in you too! Remember Jeremiah 33:3.

GOD SEES
Greatness
IN U2

Theresa C. Friday

AUTHOR • SPEAKER • COACH

About the Author

Author, entrepreneur, successful realtor, accountant, and empowerment speaker, Theresa C. Friday is a woman of many titles. However, the one she most identifies with is faithful over comer. After growing up in an ideal, two-parent family home, Friday's life dramatically changed at the age of ten. Her once happy personality became overshadowed by thoughts of unworthiness, isolation, and emotional distress. Friday found herself sinking into a deep pit of depression, and by age 18, she had attempted her first suicide. She said, "I recall crying and looking in the mirror being tormented by thoughts like: 'you're ugly', 'you're dumb', 'you're worthless', 'you have no purpose to live', and 'just kill yourself'." Her response to these tormenting accusations was to ingest several anti-depressant pills.

Instead of dying that day, Friday was "overtaken" by an anointing like [she had] never experienced before. In that moment, God sweetly reassured her of a specific life purpose that would affect millions of people, especially women. More than 16 years after that first incident, Friday found herself quarantined in a psychiatric ward battling the same demons. However, something was different this time. She recalled, "I [had] decided that enough was enough as I lay in that hospital." So, with the determination of a prized fighter, Friday prayed her way out of depression and the confines of the mental institution.

Through the power of God's grace and mercy, Friday has victoriously overcome the struggles of her past. She now considers these early incidents as the training grounds for the ministry she now shares with the world. In August 2014, she launched God Sees Greatness N U 2, LLC in memory of her late mother. This company serves as Friday's platform to discuss openly the prevalence of financial bankruptcy, mental illness, and abuse in the African American and faith-based communities.

Using her life as a roadmap, Friday offers transformative life lessons to the lost, depressed, and broken. It is her ultimate goal to educate and inspire women to pursue their personal greatness through the application of biblical principles. In the midst of this huge undertaking, Theresa Friday finds solace in her favorite scripture: "Call unto me, and I will answer thee and shew thee great and mighty things, which thou knowest not." (Jeremiah 33:3).

Booking Information

Do you need a speaker for your next event? Book Theresa C. Friday to capture your audience. Whether you need to book Theresa for a 30 – 60 minute engagement or for a workshop, she will inspire and deliver a lifelong experience that will fill your guests with the seeds of empowerment and hope!

Topics include but are not limited to:

- How to develop a solid prayer life
  - Fulfilling Purpose
- Financial Empowerment
  - Self-Motivation
  - Beating Suicide
- How to start a business or write a book
  - Overcoming Depression

Email: theresacfriday@gmail.com

Web: www.theresacfriday.com

www.ingramcontent.com/pod-product-compliance
Lightning Source LLC
LaVergne TN
LVHW021504080426
835509LV00018B/2391